THE TABLETOP LEARNING SERIES

BOX CRAFTS

Over 50 Things to Make
and Do with Boxes of Every Size
by Imogene Forte

Incentive Publications, Inc.
Nashville, Tennessee

Illustrated by Gayle Harvey
Cover illustrated by Becky Cutler
Ideas contributed by Sue Reinhardt
Edited by Sally D. Sharpe

CL
D2
745.5
c.1

Library of Congress Catalog Number 86-82933
ISBN-0-86530-123-9

THIS
BOX CRAFTS BOOK
BELONGS TO

_____

CONTENTS

LITTLE BOXES

TISSUE-TALKING BOXES

these puppets can do and say anything you want on any day

WHAT TO USE:
- individual cereal boxes
- scissors
- facial tissue or colored tissue paper
- glue
- pencil with an eraser end
- construction paper
- yarn, pipe cleaners, buttons, fabric scraps, etc.

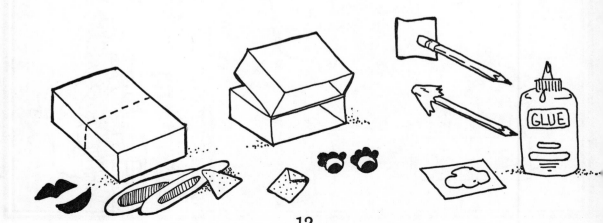

WHAT TO DO:

1. Cut 3 sides of the box to make an opening and bend it back as shown.
2. Cut tissue paper into 1" squares. Put a square over the eraser end of the pencil and dip in glue. Now attach the tissue to the box. Continue attaching squares of tissue to make hair, wool, or fur. Cover the remaining parts of the box with construction paper. Add eyes, ears, a nose, and other features as you choose. When making the mouth, remember to glue the upper lip on the top opening of the box and the lower lip on the bottom opening so the puppet can talk.

WHAT IS FUN:

Make other box puppets and stage a show for your family and friends.

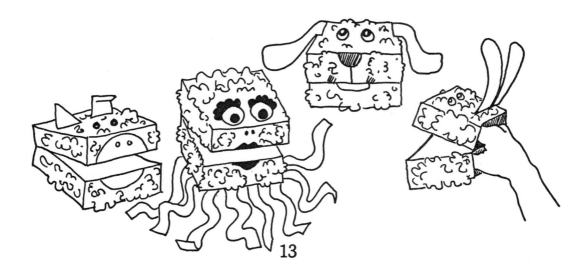

13

RAISIN BOX PUPPETS

when the raisins are gone
the fun begins

WHAT TO USE:
- small raisin boxes
- construction paper
- glue
- markers or crayons
- scissors
- yarn, buttons, fabric scraps, etc.
- craft sticks (optional)

WHAT TO DO:
1. Pull out the bottom flap of the box.
2. Carefully cut a finger-sized hole in the flap and fold the flap back in.
3. Cover the box with construction paper. (Remember to punch out the finger hole.)
4. Now give the box puppet a face, hair, and clothes using the craft materials. Perhaps you would like to make a long neck for your puppet by gluing boxes on top of each other. Use your imagination to create storybook characters or animal friends. For a sturdier puppet, glue a craft stick to the inside of the box.

WHAT IS FUN:
Ask a friend to create a puppet show with you. A covered table top makes a great stage. Act out a fairy tale or make up your own show. Invite your family and friends.

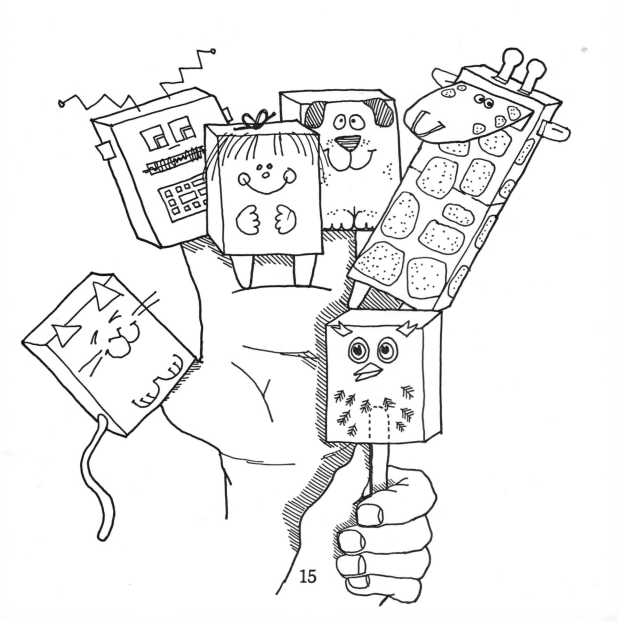

BEADS O' BOXES

WHAT TO USE:
- several small boxes (raisin boxes are good)
- tempera paint
- paintbrushes
- newspaper
- heavy thread
- needle
- scissors
- glitter (optional)

WHAT TO DO:
1. Paint the boxes in your own creative way and place them on newspaper to dry. (While they are wet, you may want to sprinkle glitter on them.)
2. Thread the needle and tie a knot at one end.
3. Run the thread through one side of the box and out the other.
4. Link all the boxes together in this way.
5. Tie the 2 ends of thread together to finish your necklace.

MAKE A MOBILE

WHAT TO USE:
- several small boxes (raisin boxes, match boxes, jewelry boxes, etc.)
- mobile base (tree branch, coat hanger, round wooden embroidery frame)
- yarn
- scissors
- markers or crayons
- glue
- construction paper
- other creative materials (seeds, noodles, etc.)

WHAT TO DO:
1. Select a base for your mobile from the suggested items.
2. Decorate the boxes with creative materials. Pick a theme to illustrate such as a holiday, birthday, seasonal or animal theme.
3. Run a piece of yarn through a hole in the top of each box and knot the yarn on the inside.
4. Attach each piece of yarn to the mobile base. Arrange the boxes in an interesting pattern. Hang your mobile in a spot where it will move in the breeze.

HIGH SCORE BOXES

whether a pro or just a beginner,
you can throw to be a winner!

WHAT TO USE:
- 6 small, light cardboard boxes (gelatin boxes or individual cereal boxes)
- white shelf paper or brown paper bags
- glue
- markers
- scissors
- sponges or knotted washcloths
- large box

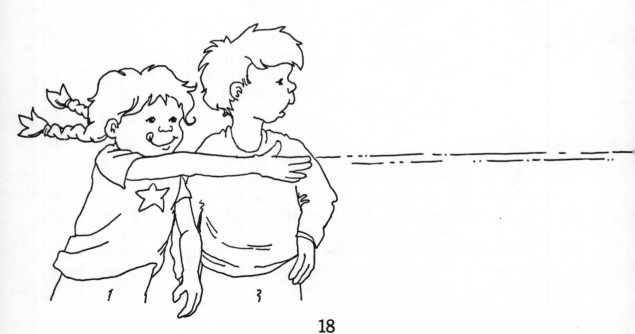

WHAT TO DO:
1. Cut enough paper to cover each box and glue the paper on the boxes individually.
2. Write the numbers 10, 15, 20, 25, 30, 35, 40 on the boxes--one on each box.
3. Put all of the boxes and the sponges or knotted washcloths in the large box for convenience.

WHAT IS FUN:
Use these rules to play High Score with a friend:

1. Agree upon the number of throws for each player.
2. Place the boxes on a table with the number side showing.
3. Agree upon a distance to throw from.
4. Take turns trying to knock the boxes over.
5. Total the scores to find the winner.

SEW-SEW BOX

make a miniature sewing kit
for someone you know who sews a bit

WHAT TO USE:
- small size cottage cheese box
- cotton or sponge
- fabric
- buttons

WHAT TO DO:
1. Wash the cottage cheese box and top with soap and dry well.
2. Glue the cotton or sponge to the outside of the top.
3. Wrap fabric completely around the top and glue the fabric in place making a pin cushion.
4. Cover the outside of the box with fabric. Pulling the fabric tightly to remove wrinkles, glue the fabric in place.
5. Stock the kit with thread, buttons, small scissors, and a package of needles. Stick straight pins in the cushion top, and put the top on the box.

WHAT IS FUN:
This miniature sewing kit makes a lovely Mother's Day or birthday gift. You also might enjoy making one to keep!

GIFT BOX WREATH

WHAT TO USE:
- lots of tiny boxes (raisin boxes, mini candy boxes, pill boxes, jewelry boxes)
- foil and gift-wrap (the fancier the better!)
- ribbon or cord
- glue
- old wreath base or cardboard circle

WHAT TO DO:
1. Wrap all the boxes in paper and tie cord or ribbon around them.
2. Arrange the boxes on the wreath base or cardboard circle and glue in place.
3. Attach a strong cord loop to the back of the wreath for hanging. Try adding a big bow to make your wreath more festive.

NOODLE DOODLE BOX

have fun and doodle, then glue on a noodle

WHAT TO USE:
- sturdy white gift box with top
- glue
- pencil
- noodles, macaroni, rice, beans

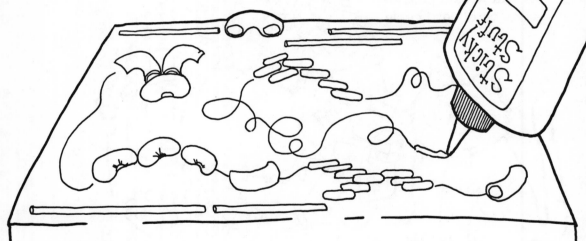

WHAT TO DO:
1. Draw an interesting doodle design all over the box and top.
2. Glue the noodles, macaroni, rice, and beans on the doodles. You might like to add a few beads and baubles if you have them. Half the fun of the noodle doodle box is deciding how to use it!

ALPHABET BOXES

spell a cheerful message --
hang it in a special place,
you're sure to put a smile
on someone's happy face!

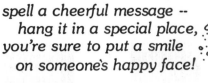

WHAT TO USE:
- gelatin or pudding boxes
- 2 solid colors of gift-wrap
- glue
- scissors
- strip of felt or ribbon
- yarn or cord

WHAT TO DO:
1. Pick a message for your banner.
2. Cover enough boxes to spell out the message with one color of gift-wrap.
3. Cut block letters out of the other gift-wrap to spell the message.
4. Glue a letter to each block.
5. Arrange the boxes on a strip of felt or ribbon and glue them in place.
6. Cut a hole in each side of the top of the banner. Run one end of a piece of cord through each hole to make a hanging loop. Tie a knot in each end to hold the loop in place.

WHAT IS FUN:
Hang your banner in a special place to greet someone with a holiday message.

IN-BETWEEN BOXES

BOX-TOPUS PIÑATA

WHAT TO USE:
- sturdy cardboard box with top
- construction paper or aluminum foil
- heavy string or wire
- masking tape
- glue
- scissors
- candy surprises
- yarn and ribbon (optional)

WHAT TO DO:
1. Fill the box ¼ full with candy.
2. Carefully cut a small hole on each side of the box and run the string through both sides. Tie the ends together tightly.
3. Tape the top to the box securely.
4. Cover the box with paper or foil.
5. Make large eyes for your box-topus and glue them on the box.

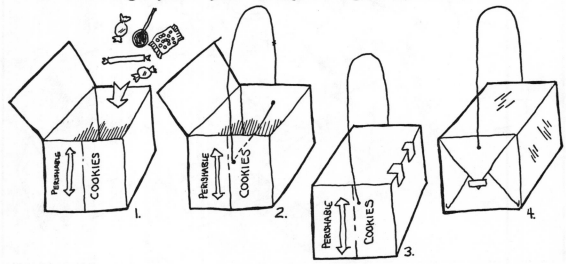

6. Cut 8 long strips of paper for legs.
7. With each strip, fold the end over, flip, and continue folding to make an accordion.
8. Tape or glue the legs to the bottom of the box. Now hang your piñata in a special place.

WHAT IS FUN:
Hang your piñata in your room for decoration and enjoy it a few days. Then invite your friends over to break the piñata. Blindfold the players, one at a time, and take turns swinging at the piñata. When it breaks, there will be candy for everyone!

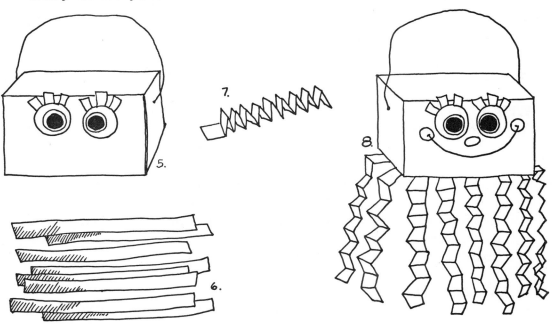

AN A-MAZE-ING BOX

WHAT TO USE:
- top or bottom of sturdy cardboard box (a shirt or sweater box is good)
- macaroni noodles
- glue
- scissors
- small ball bearing, marble, or bead
- marker or crayon

WHAT TO DO:
1. Glue the macaroni noodles to the inside of the box, end to end.
2. Make a pathway for the marble to roll along as you glue the noodles.
3. Cut a hole at the end of your macaroni maze for the marble.
4. Allow the glue to dry completely before using your maze. To make the game more difficult, make detour paths with the macaroni or cut potholes along the way.

WHAT IS FUN:
Ask a friend to play a game with you. Take turns tilting the box so the marble rolls from start to finish. Use a stopwatch to see who can do it faster!

28

SHINY SHAKERS

to shake, rattle, and roll!

WHAT TO USE:
- 2 empty boxes
  (about the size of
  individual cereal boxes)
- aluminum foil
- construction paper
- tape or glue
- dried beans
- scissors

WHAT TO DO:
1. Put ½ cup of dried beans in each box and seal the opening securely.
2. Cover the boxes with aluminum foil.
3. Cut Indian designs from construction paper and glue to the boxes.
4. Allow the glue to dry completely. Now your shiny shakers are ready to shake, rattle, and roll!

29

BOX SCULPTURE

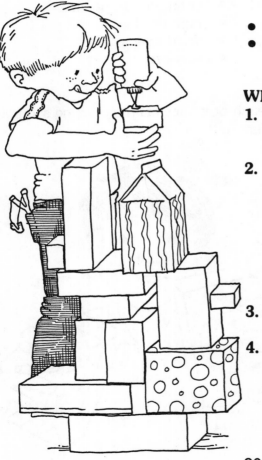

WHAT TO USE:
- many boxes of different sizes and shapes
- glue
- tempera paint, construction paper, or fabric

WHAT TO DO:

1. Gather all the empty boxes you can find. Try to collect as many different sizes and shapes as you can.

2. With all the boxes in front of you, begin making interesting designs by putting boxes side by side, on top of each other, in line horizontally, in line vertically, corner to corner, etc. Experiment with the boxes until you find a particular design that you like best.

3. Glue the boxes together to make a sculpture.

4. When the glue is completely dry, paint your sculpture with tempera paint or cover it with paper or fabric. When your sculpture is finished, give it a name and put it in a special spot in your house!

A BOX FOR BOOKS

especially nice for your desk

WHAT TO USE:
- large, sturdy shoe box
- scissors
- glue
- wallpaper or contact paper

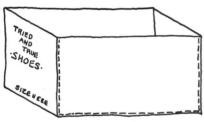

WHAT TO DO:
1. Carefully cut one side out of the shoe box.
2. Cover the remaining ends, side, and bottom, both inside and out, with contact paper or wallpaper.
3. Fill your new "box-case" with books.

FAKE LEATHER BOX

no one will suspect it's only brown paper!

WHAT TO USE:
- brown paper grocery bag
- pan of water
- several sheets of newspaper
- colored chalk
- sturdy box (candy box or cigar box works well)
- glue

WHAT TO DO:

1. Cut the bag apart to make 2 sheets.

2. Wad the sheets into balls.

3. Soak the wadded paper in water for 10 minutes.

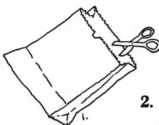

4. Remove the paper and lay it flat on newspaper.

5. Use the colored chalk to draw a design on the wet paper. Let it dry.

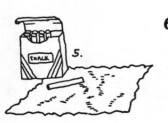

6. Cut and fit the paper over the sides, top, and inside of the box. Glue the paper in place, being careful to smooth out the wrinkles.

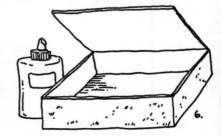

 "GRITTER" BOX

WHAT TO USE:
- sturdy box with top (empty candy box is good)
- tempera paint
- newspaper
- plastic spoons
- glue (in a squeeze bottle)
- 4 paper cups
- instant grits
- food coloring

WHAT TO DO:
1. Paint the outside of the top and bottom of the box. Let the box dry on newspaper.
2. Pour 2/3 cup of grits in each cup.
3. Add a drop of food coloring to each cup. Stir until the "gritter" is glitter.

4. When the box is completely dry, squeeze glue onto the box to make designs.
5. Sprinkle grits on the glue and wait for it to dry. Shake the left-over "gritter" into a cup. (Remember to use only one color at a time, unless you want a multi-colored design.)

WHAT IS FUN:
Keep special treasures in your "gritter" box, or use it to hold jewelry. "Gritter" boxes make great holiday gifts, too!

A BOX TO BUY

create a box that's really neat
to sell a cereal you'd like to eat

WHAT TO USE:
- large, empty cereal box
- white paper
- tape or glue
- markers or crayons
- scissors

WHAT TO DO:
1. As you read the information and study the pictures on the cereal box, think about the cereal's taste, nutritional value, and colorful box. Try to imagine how you would change the box if it contained your own top-selling cereal!

2. Cover the empty box with white paper.

3. Use markers or crayons to decorate the outside of your brand new cereal. Be sure to indicate all the necessary information. Make your box a real eye-catcher!

WHAT IS FUN:
Stage a T.V. commercial to promote your new cereal. After practicing what you will say, advertise the cereal in front of family and friends.

BIRTHDAY BOX

a cake full of surprises

WHAT TO USE:
- 3 or 4 boxes of different sizes with tops
- construction paper, wrapping paper, tissue paper, or aluminum foil
- markers or crayons
- tape or glue
- scissors
- pretzels, peppermint sticks, or other items to use for candles
- toy, candy, or other "surprises"

WHAT TO DO:
1. Put a "surprise" in each box.
2. Glue or tape the tops securely.
3. Cover each box with paper or foil.
4. Glue or tape the boxes on top of each other from largest to smallest.
5. Glue paper cutouts or draw designs on your cake. Try making slits with scissors in the boxes to put play candles in.

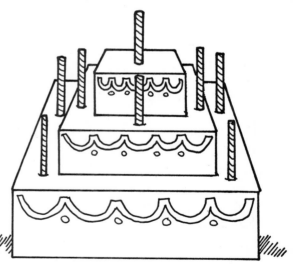

WHAT IS FUN:
Give your cake to a special family member or friend who is having a birthday. Let your friend unwrap the cake to find the special surprises in the boxes.

ORGANIZE WITH BOXES

WHAT TO USE:
- stiff cardboard
- sturdy boxes of different sizes
- fabric
- glue
- scissors

WHAT TO DO:
1. Cut the cardboard to make a wall hanging.
2. Cover the cardboard with fabric and glue the fabric in place.
3. Make two holes near the top of each side of the cardboard.
4. Cut strips of fabric to insert through the holes and tie the ends to make a hanging loop.
5. Cut the top flaps off of boxes of different sizes. Glue fabric on the boxes to cover them.
6. Arrange the boxes on the wall hanging to make an attractive design and glue them in place. When the glue dries, fill the boxes with school supplies such as pencils, pens, scissors, glue, paper, etc.

NICE DICE

WHAT TO USE:

- 2 square cardboard boxes of same size
- white construction paper or gift-wrap
- black construction paper
- tape or glue
- scissors

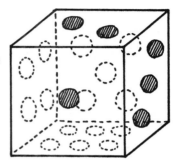

WHAT TO DO:

1. Wrap the boxes with white paper.
2. Cut 42 small circles out of black paper.
3. Glue 21 circles on each box die according to the illustration. Be sure to allow the glue to dry.

WHAT IS FUN:

Ask a friend to play a game with you. Agree upon the number of times each of you will throw the dice. Keep track of your scores as you play. The one with the highest score after the last throw is the winner!

BOX TOWN

WHAT TO USE:
- large piece of cardboard
- boxes of different shapes and sizes
- construction paper
- tape or glue

- scissors
- markers, crayons, or paint
- craft sticks
- scraps of fabric, buttons, yarn, etc.

craft sticks can be inserted into slits in the cardboard base

LIBRARY

WHAT TO DO:
1. Glue the boxes onto the cardboard to make a town. (Small boxes can be houses and large boxes can be skyscrapers.)
2. Cut out doors and windows from construction paper. (You may want to make curtains from fabric.)
3. Glue yarn to the cardboard to make roads or railroad tracks.
4. Glue craft sticks together to make fences for the town. Make your town imaginary or just like the town where you live.

TRASH BOX COLLAGE

to keep your room clean and neat

WHAT TO USE:
- large cylinder-shaped box (ice cream containers work well)
- old magazines
- glue
- scissors
- shellac (optional)

WHAT TO DO:
1. Look through the magazines and cut out pictures that tell something about you such as your favorite color or hobby.
2. Make sure the container is clean and dry. Glue the pictures on the container to make a collage. After the glue dries, you might like to shellac the trash box to give it a shiny finish!

WHAT IS FUN:
Put the trash box in a special corner of your room. Not only will it help keep your room clean, but it will also be a great conversation piece!

MAILBOX EXPRESS

a fun game to play with friends

WHAT TO USE:
- 7 boxes
- white paper
- glue or tape
- marker
- scissors
- pencils

WHAT TO DO:
1. With a marker, write the names of 7 big cities on separate pieces of paper. Glue each name to a box.
2. Have each player write the names of the 7 cities on paper and cut them out. Each player should write his or her name on the back of each strip. These are letters to be delivered.

WHAT IS FUN:
Invite some friends to play Mailbox Express with you outside. Have an adult hide the boxes secretly. Put the letters in the same chosen area (porch, swing, etc.). Each player takes a letter and searches for the right mailbox. After delivering the letter, the player runs back to get another one. The first one to deliver all 7 letters to the right boxes is the winner!

40

BUG INN

for friendly bugs only

WHAT TO USE:
- oatmeal box with top
- piece of screen wire
- pencil
- scissors
- glue
- cord
- paint or paper

WHAT TO DO:
1. Paint the box or cover it with paper.
2. Draw a window large enough to see through on the box and cut it out.
3. Fit the screen wire in the window and glue it in place.
4. With the lid on the box, make 2 holes just under the lid on each side.
5. Remove the lid and push one end of the cord in each hole. Knot each end to hold the handle in place. Now you can carry your bug inn with you!

WHAT IS FUN:
Catch some bugs and put them in your bug inn. Observe them for a while, enjoy their company, then set them free again.

VIEW BOX

WHAT TO USE:
- shoe box
- scissors
- crayons and markers
- cellophane
- construction paper
- glue and tape
- string
- pipe cleaners, clay, scraps of fabric, or other assorted "materials"

WHAT TO DO:
1. Take the top off the shoe box.
2. Cut a round hole in one end of the box for "viewing".
3. Cut a square hole in the box top, about 1½ inches from one end. Cover the hole by taping a piece of cellophane to the inside of the box. (This hole will allow the light to shine into the box.)
4. Create a scene inside the box. First, use crayons and markers to draw "background" scenery on the sides inside the box. You might like to glue scraps of fabric to the inside bottom of the box, or to color in grass or "carpet" to make a floor or ground.
5. Then, make figures and props using cardboard, construction paper, clay or pipe cleaners. Stand the figures up by gluing cardboard or popsicle sticks to the figures' backs. You can even hang objects from the top of the box with string.

6. When you have completed the scene, replace the box top, placing the light hole on the end opposite the viewing hole. Tape the top to the box. Place your view box under the light and look through the viewing hole to see your original scene!

WHAT IS FUN:
Try making an underwater or outer space scene. If you are studying a special unit at school -- a period in history, the solar system, a foreign country, etc. -- you can make a view box to show what you have learned!

OINK BANK

this box makes banking cute and funny,
so be a little piggish as you save your money!

WHAT TO USE:
- cylinder-shaped box (salt box is good)
- egg carton
- cardboard tube (toilet paper roll, paper towel roll, etc.)
- large button

- construction paper
- glue
- scissors
- pencil
- tempera paint
- brush

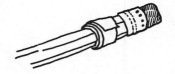

WHAT TO DO:
1. Cut the egg carton into individual sections. Use 4 sections for legs and 2 for ears.
2. Turn the empty box on its side and glue the egg carton sections to the box as shown.
3. Cut a 3-inch piece of cardboard tubing. Glue a button to the end of the tube.
4. Carefully cut a hole in the front end of the box. Make the hole a little smaller than the circumference of the tube.

5. Insert the tube in the hole. Now you have a removable snout for inserting or removing coins.
6. When the glue is dry, paint your bank.
7. Cut eyes out of construction paper and glue them to the front of the box. Try making curly eyelashes and a curly tail by wrapping a thin strip of paper around a pencil and holding it tightly for a minute. (The tail can be inserted into the salt box's spout.) Glue on the special features to give your pig its own personality!

BARNYARD BOX

from a shoe box to a stable

WHAT TO USE:
- large shoe box
- piece of corrugated cardboard
- glue or tape
- scissors
- straw or craft sticks (optional)
- flat cardboard (optional)

WHAT TO DO:
1. Cut out one side of a shoe box and glue it to the back of the other side so that it sticks up 2 inches.

2. Cut a piece of the corrugated cardboard to use for a roof. Make it larger than the shoe box so there is some overhang.
3. Glue the roof to the top of the box.
4. Fold pieces of the corrugated board to make stalls and put them in the corners of the stable. You may want to glue grass or straw on the roof. Craft sticks glued together make great fences. (You can glue your stable to a piece of flat cardboard for a base.)

WHAT IS FUN:

Shelter or feed your toy animals in the barnyard box. You may want to create a special scene around the stable.

47

MONSTER MASKS

and other disguises

WHAT TO USE:
- boxes
- scissors
- tape
- markers
- junk materials

WHAT TO DO:

1. Think about who or what you would like to be

   > *A dinosaur, a robot, a dragon mean,*
   >> *an octopus, a cowboy, or even a queen . . .*
   >
   > *Give your imagination a fling --*
   >> *it's only make believe, so you can be anything!*

2. Select a box.
3. Cut out spaces to allow you to see and breathe. Use junk materials to "fashion your face ".

WHIZ KID BOXES

questions are answers and answers are questions

WHAT TO USE:
- 2 white gift boxes
  of the same size
- felt tip pens

- 20 5" x 7" index cards
- scissors
- reference books

WHAT TO DO:
1. Print "Question" on one box and "Answer" on the other.
2. Use the reference books to find interesting facts. Example: Q. What is the largest living mammal? A. The Blue Whale.

3. Write a question on one half of an index card and the answer on the other half.
4. Cut each card down the middle using a zigzag or uneven line.
5. Put the question cards in the question box and the answer cards in the answer box.

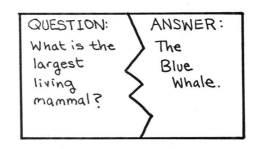

WHAT IS FUN:

1. Ask a friend to play a game with you.
2. You take the question box and give your friend the **answer box.**
3. Pick a question from the box and read it to your friend.
4. Your friend looks at the answer cards, picks the answer that he or she thinks is right and reads it to you.
5. If the cards match, your friend is right and keeps both cards. If the cards do not match, your friend is wrong and must put them back.
6. Now let your friend pick an answer from the answer box and read it to you.
7. After looking at your question cards, pick the question that you think is a match and read it to your friend.
8. If the cards match, you are right and may keep both cards. If you are wrong, put the cards back.
9. When all the cards have been matched, see who has the most!

Note: Older family members may make the questions and answers for you to make the game more difficult. The neat thing about this game is that the more you play, the smarter you get!

PATRIOTIC MAILBOX

WHAT TO USE:
- oatmeal box
- shoe box
- construction paper or
  poster paints

- tape or glue
- scissors
- paper brad

WHAT TO DO:
1. Remove the top of the shoe box.
2. Cut out a flagpole for the mailbox from the top of the shoe box.
3. Make a copy of your country's flag out of construction paper and glue it to the pole.
4. Carefully make a small slit in the bottom of the pole and in the side of the box.
5. Attach the flagpole to the box with the brad so that the flag moves up and down.
6. Cut the oatmeal box in half lengthwise.
7. Tape or glue one half of the oatmeal box to the top rim of the shoe box.
8. Paint the mailbox or cover it with construction paper. You might like to paint the name of your country on the side of the box for decoration.

WHAT IS FUN:
Take your mailbox to school on a national holiday. Ask your teacher's permission to do the following activity. Have your classmates write why they love their country on pieces of paper and put the papers in the mailbox throughout the day. Take the papers out of the box at the end of the day, read them to the class and then talk about them. This is a great way to celebrate a special holiday!

POW-WOW-BOX

beat your own drum

WHAT TO USE:
- oatmeal box with top
- fabric
- yarn
- hole punch
- scissors
- construction paper or poster paint
- tape or glue

WHAT TO DO:
1. Remove the top of the box and paint or cover the box with construction paper.
2. Punch a hole 3 inches from the top on opposite sides of the box.
3. Run a long piece of yarn through the holes and tie the ends securely so the drum will hang around your neck.
4. Cut 2 circles out of fabric. Make them larger than the top of the box.

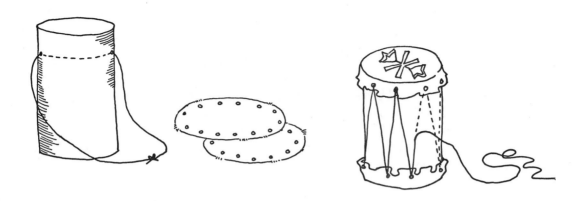

5. Put the top back on the box. With the circles together, punch holes around the edge, 2 inches apart.
6. Place one circle over the box's top and the other under the bottom. (A few drops of glue might help to keep the fabric in place.)
7. Run a long piece of yarn through a hole in the bottom fabric piece and knot it. Weave the yarn through the top fabric and back through the bottom fabric. Continue this weaving pattern all around the box. Tie a knot at the end. Decorate your drum with Indian designs cut from construction paper.

WHAT IS FUN:
The eraser end of a blunt pencil and a spoon make great drumsticks. Let a friend clap a rhythm for you to echo on your drum.

V.S.P. BOX

a box full of wishes for a very special person

Think of a very special person you would like to send a box of good wishes.
Maybe you know someone who is having a birthday or is in the hospital. You
might just want to say "I love you" to your parents or a special teacher. Now
think of enough good wishes to send your special friend for each day of 1
week, 2 weeks, or even a month.

WHAT TO USE:
- empty tissue box
- solid color gift-wrap,
  butcher paper or fabric
- glue
- scissors

- old magazines and newspapers
- strips of writing paper
- pencil
- yarn or ribbon

WHAT TO DO:

1. Cover the box with wrapping paper.
2. Cut pictures, words, and captions from newspapers and magazines to glue on the box which describe your special person or illustrate your theme (birthday, get well, holiday greetings, etc.). Add original drawings or phrases to personalize the box.
3. Write wishes, riddles and rhymes, or special messages on strips of paper.
4. Roll each strip of paper into a scroll and tie it with ribbon or yarn. Put the scrolls in the box and send the box to your very special person. Sometimes it may be fun to have other people write wishes for the box, too!

BOX KAZOO

WHAT TO USE:
- waxed paper or foil box
- rubber band
- waxed paper
- pencil

WHAT TO DO:
1. Cut both ends out of the box.
2. Cut a piece of waxed paper to cover one end of the box and extend the paper over each side an inch or 2 (see illustration).
3. Hold the waxed paper in place with a rubber band, making

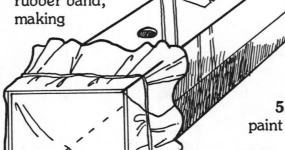

sure the rubber band is tight.
4. Use a pencil to punch a hold in the box about an inch from the covered end.
5. If you want a fancy kazoo, paint the box or cover it with paper.

WHAT IS FUN:
Hold the open end of the kazoo to your mouth. Pucker your lips and sing or hum a favorite tune. You will be surprised at the sound you will make! Practicing will help you to develop your own special kazoo sound that will impress your friends.

TERRIFIC TERRARIUM

WHAT TO USE:
- plastic wrap or clear acetate
- ½ gallon milk carton
- scissors
- tape
- soil and pebbles
- long-handled spoon
- plant

WHAT TO DO:
1. Wash out the milk carton with soap.
2. Cut out rectangular windows from all 4 sides of the carton.
3. Cut 4 pieces of plastic wrap or acetate to fit over each window. Tape the plastic wrap in place.
4. Place a layer of pebbles in the bottom of the carton.
5. Pour a thick layer of soil over the pebbles.
6. Make a hole in the soil with the spoon. Put the plant in the hole and pat the dirt around the plant firmly with a spoon. Be sure to cover the roots.
7. Close the top of the carton and tape it securely.

WHAT IS FUN:
Watch your plant grow through the clear windows. If too much moisture forms, untape the top of the carton to let air in. If your terrarium is successful, try making another one for a shut-in's windowsill.

LOOK WHAT ELSE YOU CAN DO WITH MILK CARTONS

Milk cartons are marvelous for all kinds of arts and crafts projects, and they come in so many different sizes.

Not only are milk cartons sturdy, but they're also waterproof. Just remember to **always** wash the cartons with soap and dry them thoroughly before beginning a project.

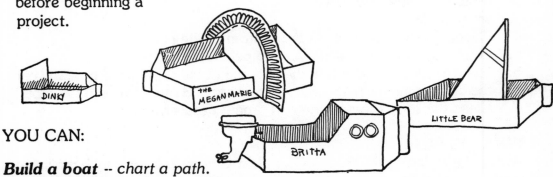

YOU CAN:

Build a boat -- *chart a path.*
Set sail in a puddle or bubble bath.

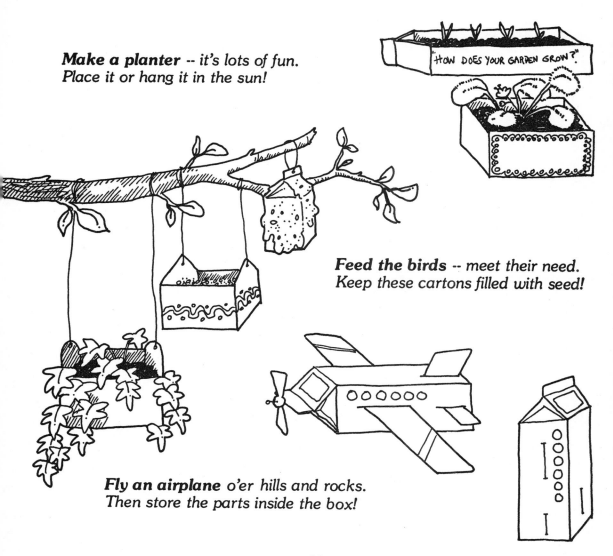

Make a planter -- it's lots of fun.
Place it or hang it in the sun!

"HOW DOES YOUR GARDEN GROW?"

Feed the birds -- meet their need.
Keep these cartons filled with seed!

Fly an airplane o'er hills and rocks.
Then store the parts inside the box!

61

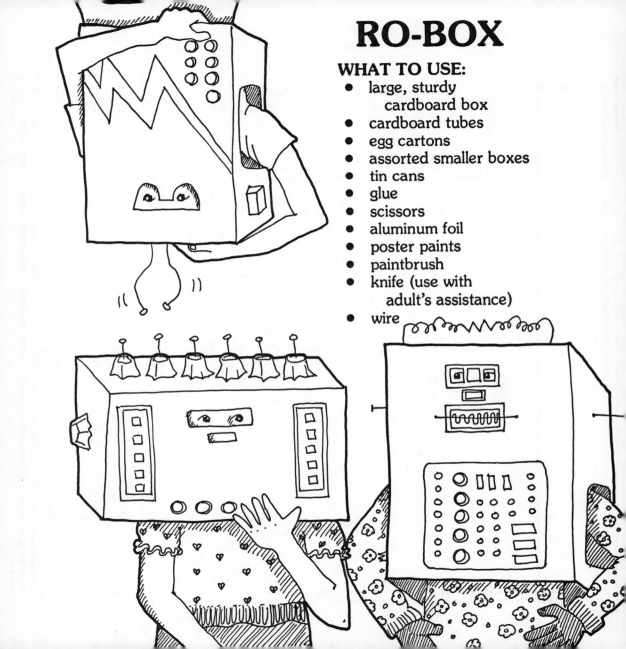

RO-BOX

WHAT TO USE:

- large, sturdy cardboard box
- cardboard tubes
- egg cartons
- assorted smaller boxes
- tin cans
- glue
- scissors
- aluminum foil
- poster paints
- paintbrush
- knife (use with adult's assistance)
- wire

WHAT TO DO:

1. Put the box over your head. Have an adult draw spaces for eye and arm holes.
2. Take off the box and let an adult help you cut out the holes.
3. Paint your ro-box a bright color.
4. Use the assorted materials to glue on buttons, antennae, and any complicated devices. Objects covered with aluminum foil give your ro-box an out-of-this-world look. Use your imagination!

WHAT IS FUN:

While you wear your ro-box, pretend you are a real robot. Talk with a robot voice and take orders from a friend.

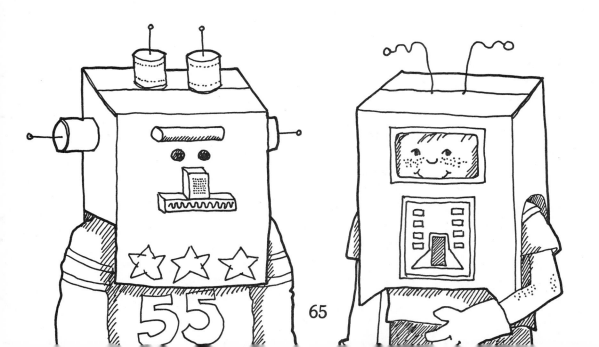

BOX-A-VISION

WHAT TO USE:
- glue
- marker
- scissors or knife
- wire coat hanger
- large, sturdy cardboard box
- paint, aluminum foil, or paper (optional)
- little boxes, bottle caps, egg cartons, Styrofoam balls, etc.

WHAT TO DO:
1. On the side opposite the open end of the box, use a marker to trace a cutting line for the picture screen. Ask an adult to help you cut out the screen.
2. Unwind a wire hanger to make antennae.
3. Glue egg carton sections on the top of the box. Insert the antennae in the egg cartons.
4. Paint or cover your T.V. (optional)
5. Make knobs and dials with little boxes, bottle caps, or other materials. (Cover the dials and knobs with aluminum foil to make them look like metal.) Glue the knobs and dials on the box.

WHAT IS FUN:
Crawl inside your T.V. and turn the knob. Create your own show and commercials. (Turn to page 34 for a fun activity to use with your T.V.) Invite your friends over to watch your special programs!

PUPPETS ON PARADE

in your own theater!

WHAT TO USE:
- large cardboard box (refrigerator or freezer box)
- scissors
- tempera paint
- big paintbrush
- markers
- fabric
- string
- tape

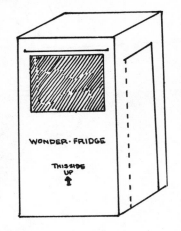

WHAT TO DO:
1. Stand the box upright and cut a door in the side of the box.
2. Cut a large window for the stage in the top half of the front side.
3. Make a small hole at the top of each side of the window.
4. Cut enough string to run through both holes and tie on the inside.

68

5. After cutting a piece of fabric to fit the window, tape the fabric over the string. Now hang the curtain by feeding the string through the holes and tieing the ends inside the box.
6. Paint the theater a bright color and use markers to decorate it.

WHAT IS FUN:

Use different kinds of boxes to make puppets for your theater. Make up a play or act out your favorite play for your family and friends.

THE SUGAR·BEAR·THEATER

LITTLE RED RIDING HOOD

ACT 2

A HOUSE FOR ALL SEASONS

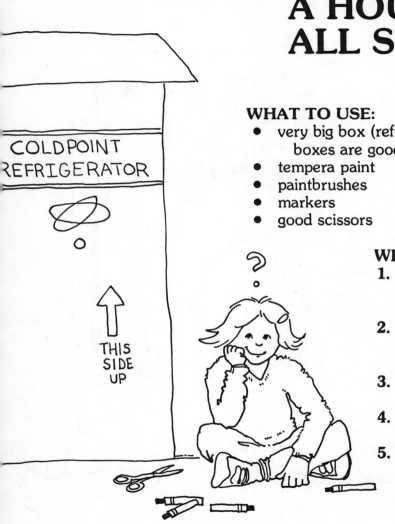

WHAT TO USE:
- very big box (refrigerator, freezer, and stove boxes are good)
- tempera paint
- paintbrushes
- markers
- good scissors

WHAT TO DO:
1. Stand the box upright and think about the house you want to make.
2. Draw a door big enough for you to walk through on the front of the box.
3. Draw a window on each side of the box.
4. Carefully cut out the door and windows with scissors.
5. Paint the house. Personalize your house by drawing or painting shutters, window panes, or other features.

70

WHAT IS FUN:
Be creative. Your house can be a club house, a "toy" house, a prop for creative dramas, or just a hideaway.

BOWLING BOX

now you can bowl on your own floor

WHAT TO USE:
- large, sturdy box
- scissors
- tape
- markers
- 4 tennis balls

WHAT TO DO:
1. With the box upright, draw 4 arches big enough for a tennis ball to go through.
2. Make each arch narrower than the one before it.
3. Carefully cut out the arches.
4. Above the arches write 1 - 4, with 1 being the widest and 4 being the narrowest.
5. Place the box on the floor and get ready to bowl!

WHAT IS FUN:
Ask a friend to bowl with you. Take turns trying to roll the tennis balls through the arches. Agree upon the distance to bowl from and the number of times each player will bowl. The player with the highest score is the winner.

LOOK WHAT ELSE YOU CAN DO WITH BIG, BIG BOXES

1. Make a pretend boat -- put it in motion, roll with the waves in a rocky ocean!

2. Build a fort -- box yourself in, stage friendly battles with a favorite friend.

3. Set up a lemonade stand -- charge a fair price; for keeping your goods, big boxes are nice!

VERY GOOD HOME MADE SECRET RECIPE
LEMONADE
10¢

DO NOT LITTER

4. Stage a performance -- call friends around, unfold a box and paint your background.

HEIDI ACT 1

5. *Decorate a toy box, and after you play, keep your room tidy -- put toys away.*

My Toys AND OTHER GOOD JUNK

PRIVATE KEEP OUT!

ANNE'S SPECIAL PLACE

6. *Design a box just for you -- a special place to hide, when you want to be alone -- simply crawl inside.*

WHAT'S IN THE BOX?

I am a small box -- I smell good, indeed
   in me you'll find something all of us need.
It's sometimes by itself and sometimes on a rope.
   I am a box and in me is _____ .

I am a flat box -- I'm carried aroun'.
   I am delivered all over town.
I carry something spicy to eat,
   within me is _____ , a favorite treat.

I contain something nutritiously right,
   sometimes it's dark and sometimes it's light.
Cows appreciate me and people do, too,
   drinking what is in me is good for you.
I'm not made of rubber, cotton, or silk,
   I am a carton and I contain _____ .

I am a box -- I contain sticks,
　guess again if you think I hold toothpicks.
Each stick is powerful though it is small,
　some have left forests with no trees at all!
So use them carefully, without a doubt,
　and put up the _____ when kids are about.

I am a box you have seen before,
　I carry something you buy at a store.
What you find inside comes in a pair,
　they smell good when new -- they're something you wear.
When you see lots of them -- it's hard to choose,
　it's really special owning new _____ .

INDEX